Grandad

Mom said Grandad was coming
to live with us.
"Why does he have to live
at *our* house?" I asked.

"Grandad gets lonely on his own," said Mom.
"I'm on my own too and he wants to help me."

"You're not on your own.
You've got us kids," I said.
"And Grandad had better not
boss me around."

Grandad had the spare room.
I had to carry a lot of his things in
and I was dying to ask
about some of them.
There was this little box
that was really heavy.
There was a fishing-rod
and a box of fishing-tackle.

When I was carrying one of the boxes,
Grandad said, "Don't drop that, son.
Those are my war memories."

I really wanted to take off the lid,
but I didn't even ask about it.
He could keep his war
and everything else to himself.

When Grandad was asleep in an armchair,
he looked old.
But when he was awake,
you forgot he was old.

Peter was always on his knee saying,
"Tell me another story, Grandad."

I'd pretend I wasn't listening,
but he did tell very good stories.

8

"Are you coming fishing, son?"
he asked one Saturday.

Of course I wanted to, but I said,
"No, thank you.
I'm going to a movie with David."

"On a day like this!"
Grandad looked surprised.

Peter went with him.
I got mad listening
to the two of them
fussing about making
their sandwiches.
I slammed the door
and went
to David's house.

"We used Grandad's secret bait,"
Peter said when he showed me
all the fish they had caught.

Mom liked having Grandad
to help in the garden.
She liked knowing he was in the house
when she was at work or out at night.
Some nights I couldn't turn on TV
because she and Grandad sat and talked
or played cards.
Judy and Peter sometimes joined in.

"Grandad needs other friends too," Mom said. "Adam, you must take him to meet Mrs. Timlin. She's about the same age as Grandad."

My face went red.
I even felt a bit sorry for Grandad.
He was a *man*.
Mrs. Timlin was a *woman*.
I was sure Grandad didn't want a woman for a friend.

"Aw, Mom," I said,
"I don't want to do that."

Mom looked at me.
"It seems there's a lot
you don't want to do
these days," she said.

One night Grandad brought out the heavy box.
It was full of coins
from countries he had been to years ago.
Grandad started telling Judy and Peter
stories about all the different places.

"Hey, turn off the TV
and come and listen, Adam," said Judy.

I stared at Judy,
but I was actually talking to Grandad.
"I want to watch TV,
not look at dumb old coins," I said rudely.

"That's OK, son," said Grandad.
He smiled kindly.
"That's fine with me."

"It's not fine with *me*,"
said Mom's voice at the door.
"You apologize, Adam, and go to your room."

The next day Mom made me take Grandad
to meet Mrs. Timlin.
I felt really silly,
but Grandad and Mrs. Timlin got along fine.
They didn't go red or anything.

I sat and watched them, and suddenly I knew
that old people didn't mind
who their friends were —
men, women, old people, young people.
I guess they've been around long enough
to practice getting along with everybody.

I got used to Grandad being at our house.
He didn't change things much.
He made friends with lots of people.
When they all went out,
I sometimes wished
Grandad was around to play cards with me.
You should have heard
the stories he could tell!

David and I asked him to come to our class
when we were learning about wars.
You could have heard a pin drop
when he told his stories.
I felt really proud of my Grandad.